Destination Detectives

Mexico

North America

Europe

Asia

Africa

MEXICO

South America

Australasia

A Gift for You

To: Mr. Green's Class

From: Sofie Brown

BOOKFAIRS BY BOOKENDS

11/6/07

© 2006 Raintree
Published by Raintree,
A division of Reed Elsevier, Inc.
Chicago, Illinois

Customer Service   888–363–4266

Visit our website at www.raintreelibrary.com

Printed and bound in China
by South China Printing Company

10 09 08 07 06
10 9 8 7 6 5 4 3 2 1

**Library of Congress Cataloging-in-
Publication Data**
Green, Jen.
  Mexico / Jen Green.
    p. cm. -- (Destination detectives)
  Includes bibliographical references.
  ISBN 1-4109-2463-7 (lib. bdg.) –
  ISBN 1-4109-2470-X (pbk.)
  1. Mexico--Description and travel--Juvenile literature. 2.
Mexico--Geography--Juvenile literature. I. Title. II. Series.
  F1216.5.G73 2005
  917.2--dc22
                          2005011557

This leveled text is a version of *Freestyle:
Destination Detectives: Mexico*

Acknowledgments
The author and publishers are grateful to the following
for permission to reproduce copyright material:
ABPL p. 18 (Tony Robins); Action Plus pp. 26-27 (Neil
Tingle); Alamy Images pp. 20r (Brian Atkinson), 43
(britishcolumbiaphotos.com), 20l (D. Hurst), 34 (Danita
Delimont), 30-31 (John Arnold Images), 38-39 (PCL), 12-13
(Stock Connection); Bridgeman Art Library pp. 10 (Father
Hidalgo (mural), Orozco, Jose Clemente (1883-1949) /
Government Palace, Guadalajara, Mexico, Mexicolore), 10-11
(Museo Nacional de Historia, Mexico City, Mexico); Corbis
pp. 8 (Bettmann), 38 (Bob Krist), 24 (Bohemian Nomad
Picturemakers), 32-33 (Carl & Ann Purcell), pp. 9l, 22-23, 41
(Charles & Josette Lenars), pp. 16-17, 18-19, 21, 33, 40, 42
(Danny Lehman), 29 (Gerald French), 35 (Gideon Mendel),
5 (Gunter Marx Photography), 9r (Historical Picture Archive),
13 (Kevin Schafer), 12, 36 (Macduff Everton), 16 (Nik
Wheeler), 15 (Owen Franken), 26 (Pablo San Juan), 28 (Phil
Schermeister), 31 (Randy Faris), 14-15 (Reuters), 36-37
(Robert Holmes), 42-43 (Stephen Frink), 24-25 (Steve Starr), 7t
(Tom Bean); Corbis Royalty Free pp. 7b, 28-29;
Harcourt Education Ltd pp. 4-5, 6 (John Miller);
www.visitmexicopress.com pp. 23, 30.

Cover photograph of cactus reproduced with permission of
Corbis/B.S.P.I..

Illustrations by Kamae Design.

Every effort has been made to contact copyright holders
of any material reproduced in this book. Any omissions will
be rectified in subsequent printings if notice is given to the
publishers.

The paper used to print this book comes from
sustainable resources.

Contents

Any words appearing in the text in bold, **like this**, are explained in the glossary. You can also look out for them in the Word Bank at the bottom of each page.

You wake up in a hotel room to the sound of music and singing. You look out. You see a narrow street with brightly colored buildings.

Strolling players

A small band of musicians is strolling down the street. There are two men strumming guitars. A third is playing a violin. They are singing a sad song with Spanish words.

Mariachi music

Mariachi bands play to crowds in town squares and cafés all over Mexico. The songs are played with guitars, trumpets, and violins. Musicians often wear traditional costume (see photo on page 5).

> Here is a typical street in central Puebla. This is where your journey begins!

WORD BANK   sombrero large hat with a wide brim, often worn by Mexican men

Where are you?

The musicians' clothes give you a clue to where you are. They are all wearing **sombreros**. Sombreros are hats with broad brims. They are also wearing cowboy boots.

This must be Mexico! These musicians are one of Mexico's famous *mariachi* bands.

You are in the city of Puebla. Puebla is located in Mexico's Central Highlands. You are just in time for a big fiesta (festival). The band is warming up.

Ponchos and sombreros

Ponchos are traditional clothes worn by Mexican farmworkers. A poncho is a square of woven cloth. It has a hole to put your head through. Sombreros are wide-brimmed hats. They protect the head from the sun.

Ponchos keep off the rain. They also keep people warm in chilly weather.

mariachi band of Mexican street musicians. They sing and play violins, guitars, and trumpets.

You look through a tourist brochure. It has photos and a map of Mexico's many regions.

The land

In the north, Mexico shares a wide **border** with the United States. The country gets much narrower in the south. Southern Mexico shares a shorter border with Guatemala and Belize.

There are two large **peninsulas**. A peninsula is a piece of land that juts out into the sea. Baja California is a long, thin peninsula in northern Mexico. The Yucatán Peninsula is in the southeast.

Where do people live?

Northern Mexico is mainly a dry, bare land. Few people live there. Most people live in the towns and cities of the Central Plateau. This is where Puebla is. The far south and the Yucatán Peninsula have fewer towns and villages.

Mexico fact file

POPULATION:
104.9 million

AREA:
756,066 square miles (1,958,202 square kilometers)

CAPITAL:
Mexico City

LANGUAGES:
Spanish is the official language. There are over 50 Mexican Indian languages.

The Yucatán Peninsula has dense, wet forests called rain forests. These rain forests are home to some unusual plants and animals.

WORD BANK   border   imaginary line dividing one country from another

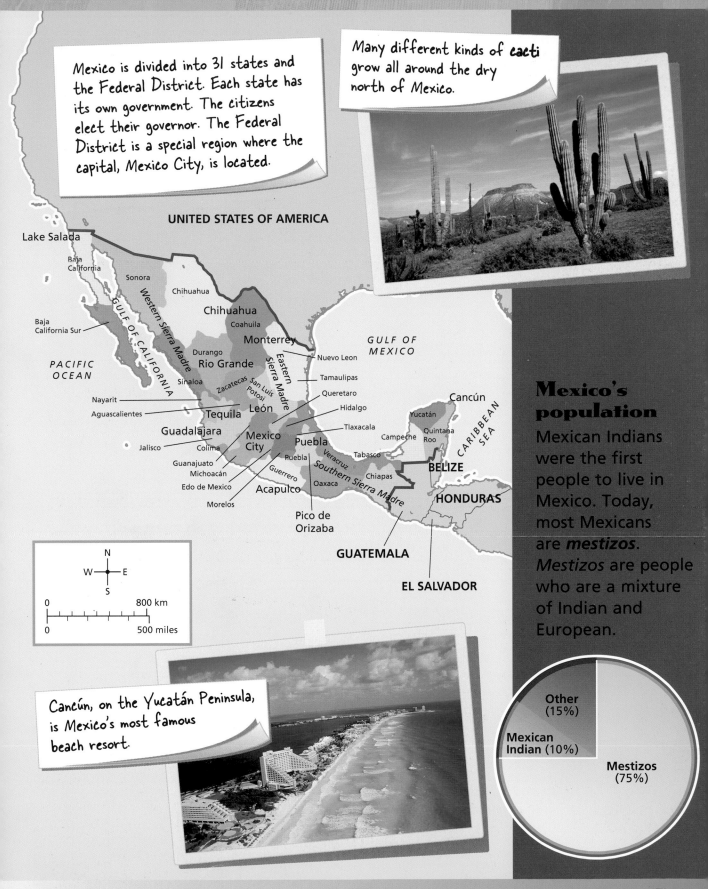

Mexico is divided into 31 states and the Federal District. Each state has its own government. The citizens elect their governor. The Federal District is a special region where the capital, Mexico City, is located.

Many different kinds of **cacti** grow all around the dry north of Mexico.

UNITED STATES OF AMERICA

Lake Salada

Baja California

Sonora

Chihuahua

Chihuahua

Coahuila

Baja California Sur

GULF OF CALIFORNIA

Western Sierra Madre

Monterrey

PACIFIC OCEAN

Durango

Rio Grande

Nuevo Leon

Eastern Sierra Madre

GULF OF MEXICO

Sinaloa

Tamaulipas

Zacatecas

San Luis Potosí

Queretaro

Nayarit

Aguascalientes

Tequila

León

Hidalgo

Cancún

Yucatán

Tlaxacala

Quintana Roo

Campeche

CARIBBEAN SEA

Guadalajara

Mexico City

Puebla

Tabasco

Jalisco

Colima

Puebla

Veracruz

BELIZE

Guanajuato

Guerrero

Southern Sierra Madre

Chiapas

Michoacán

Oaxaca

HONDURAS

Edo de Mexico

Acapulco

Morelos

Pico de Orizaba

GUATEMALA

EL SALVADOR

Mexico's population

Mexican Indians were the first people to live in Mexico. Today, most Mexicans are *mestizos*. *Mestizos* are people who are a mixture of Indian and European.

N
W — E
S

0   800 km

0   500 miles

Cancún, on the Yucatán Peninsula, is Mexico's most famous beach resort.

Other (15%)

Mexican Indian (10%)

Mestizos (75%)

peninsula piece of land with water on three sides

History

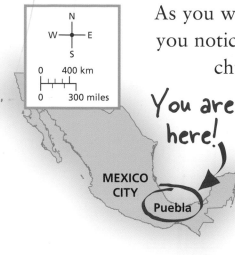

You are here!

MEXICO CITY

Puebla

Human sacrifice

The Aztecs made human **sacrifices** to their sun god. They killed people and offered their hearts to the god (see below). The Aztecs thought they had to do this so the sun would rise each day.

As you walk around Puebla, you notice a strange hill with a church on top. Someone tells you this is the Great Pyramid of Cholula. It is the remains of an ancient temple.

Mexico has been home to many great **civilizations**. These civilizations built amazing cities. Some of these ancient cities are still standing.

The Aztecs

The Aztecs were the last great Indian civilization. They ruled most of Mexico from the 1300s to the 1520s. The Aztecs were conquered by soldiers from Spain in western Europe. These Spanish soldiers were called **conquistadors** (see panel on page 9).

New Spain

The Spanish took over the Aztec land and made it bigger. They called this land New Spain. New Spain included most of Central America and large areas of the United States. The Spanish built towns and cities all over Mexico. They looked like the towns and cities in Spain.

WORD BANK   civilization very organized society that has grown in a particular country or region

The Spanish conquest

In 1519 a Spanish soldier named Hernán Cortés arrived in Mexico. He brought men, guns, and cannons. It took Cortés and his men less than three years to conquer the Aztecs. They were called conquistadors.

This painting shows Hernán Cortés (left) meeting the Aztec ruler, Montezuma. Montezuma was killed in 1520.

The Great Pyramid of Cholula was once the largest temple in Central America. A church was later built on top of it.

sacrifice someone or something that is killed and offered to a god

You visit Puebla's Museum of the Revolution. Here you find out about Mexico's recent history.

The cry from Dolores

In 1810 Father Miguel Hidalgo made a famous speech. He spoke from his church in Dolores in central Mexico. Hidalgo urged Mexicans to drive out the Spanish. This speech started the **rebellion** that won Mexico its freedom.

Spanish rule

The Spanish ruled Mexico for 300 years. Life was hard for the Mexicans. They had to work on the land or in mines. These mines kept Spain supplied with silver and gold.

In 1810 the Mexicans began fighting against their Spanish rulers. Mexico finally won freedom from Spain in 1821.

Hidalgo's speech is known as the *grito de Dolores*, or the "cry from Dolores."

WORD BANK   independence country free from control of another country

Early years of independence

Mexico's first century of **independence** was difficult. It fought wars with Britain, France, Spain, and the United States. Mexico lost about half its land to the United States.

In 1877 Porfirio Díaz became president of Mexico. He was a harsh ruler who had complete power. In 1910 Mexicans began fighting against Díaz's control. This is known as the Mexican **Revolution**. Diaz ran away to France in 1911. Fighting ended in 1917 with victory for the people.

France invaded Mexico in 1862. Mexicans defeated the French at the Battle of Puebla, seen here. However, the French defeated the Mexicans later that year.

rebellion when a group of people join together to fight against the people who are in power

Climate and Geography

Puebla is ringed by mountains. You look at a map to see what the rest of Mexico is like.

Mountains and plateaus

Mexico is mountainous. More than half the country is above 3,300 feet (1,000 meters). There are three long chains of mountains. These are the western, eastern, and southern Sierra Madre (see map, page 7).

The large, high area in between the Sierra Madres is called the Central **Plateau**. Puebla is in the Central Plateau.

Underground Mexico

Mexico has lots of amazing cave systems (see below). Many of them are in the Yucatán Peninsula.

Rivers and lowlands

Mexico's longest river is the Río Bravo. It is sometimes called the Río Grande. The Río Grande forms most of the **border** with the United States.

The biggest lowlands in Mexico are along the Gulf Coast and the Yucatán Peninsula.

There are many underground rivers in the Yucatán. The roofs of these underground rivers have collapsed in places. This creates rocky pools called *cenotes*.

Cenotes (pools) like this one have clear blue waters. ▼

Copper Canyon

The *Barranca del Cobre* (Copper **Canyon**) is one of Mexico's most dramatic sights. It is made up of five linked canyons in the western Sierra Madre.

▲ The Copper Canyon is wider and deeper than the Grand Canyon in the United States.

canyon deep valley with steep sides that has been formed by running water

Birth of a volcano

Paricutín is Mexico's youngest volcano. *Paricutín* began life in 1943. It first appeared as a smoking mound in a farmer's field. Today *Paricutín* is a towering mountain. It is over 9,200 feet (2,800 meters) high.

Volcanoes and earthquakes

What was that? For a second the ground seemed to shake. But no one took much notice. Someone says it was a **tremor**. A tremor is a small earthquake.

In the Pacific Ocean, there is a deep trench, or ditch. The trench is where two giant sections of the Earth's crust meet and push together. This action causes volcanoes to **erupt** in Mexico. It also causes earthquakes within the country. Mexico often gets small tremors. Sometimes it gets major earthquakes.

The name *Popocatépetl* means "Old Smoky" in a local Indian language. ▶

WORD BANK   erupt to release lava and ash

Smoking volcano

A line of volcanic mountains runs west to east across Mexico. These mountains include two volcanoes that tower over Puebla. They are *Iztaccíhuatl*, or Izta, and *Popocatépetl*, or Popo. Izta is not expected to erupt again. But Popo is **active**. You often see smoke rising from the mountain.

A major earthquake hit Mexico City in 1985. It destroyed many buildings and killed more than 6,000 people.

---

active likely to erupt sometime in the future

Weather in Mexico

The noon sun is fierce in Puebla. Everyone wears hats and sunglasses. Many people take a nap after lunch. It cools down in the late afternoon.

Different climates

The hottest areas in Mexico are the lowlands. Mexico's coolest areas are in the high mountains. The Central **Plateau** is between these two. It has warm summers and cool winters.

Parts of southeast Mexico get up to 157 inches (400 centimeters) of rain each year. This high rainfall allows thick forests to grow.

WORD BANK   plateau area of high, flat land
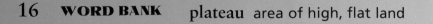

Rainfall

Puebla gets plenty of rain. But many parts of Mexico get very little rainfall. As a result, more than half the country is covered with desert or scrubland. Scrubland is land where small trees and bushes grow.

Parts of southern Mexico, however, get too much rain. Heavy summer rain in Chiapas and Tabasco (see map, page 7) sometimes causes huge floods.

(see map, page 7)

Hurricane season

In late summer **hurricanes** sometimes hit the coast of southern Mexico. These tropical storms start out at sea. They can cause great destruction when they move inland.

Pico de Orizaba is Mexico's highest mountain. The peak is always covered in snow.

hurricane fierce storm with very high winds

Food and Culture

It's evening now and time to think about food. Mexican food is a mixture of Spanish and Mexican Indian cooking. Spicy Mexican dishes are popular in many countries.

Tortillas

Mexico's main food is corn (maize). Corn is used to make flat pancakes called tortillas. These can be filled or topped with cheese, meat, and spices.

On the menu

- **Tacos:** tortillas rolled around fillings such as cheese, beans, vegetables, or spicy meat
- **Tostadas:** flat tortillas toasted and piled with toppings
- **Guacamole:** avocado dip
- **Chiles rellenos:** green chili peppers stuffed with cheese or meat.

This taco is served with lettuce, avocado, and sour cream.

Beans and chilies

Beans and chilies are used in many dishes. One of the most famous Mexican dishes is chili con carne. This is meat and beans served in a hot chili sauce.

Foods of Mexico

Many Mexican foods are now used in cooking around the world. Chocolate, vanilla, and chili peppers are Mexican foods. Tomatoes, avocados, beans, and peanuts also come from Mexico.

There are many kinds of tasty Mexican snacks. You can buy them at almost any time of day.

Fiesta day

The next day is May 5, or *Cinco de Mayo*. This is a time of celebration. On this day in 1862, the Mexicans beat the French at the Battle of Puebla. All of Mexico celebrates this victory. The biggest celebrations are here in Puebla.

Celebrations begin

Early on fiesta day, the market opens in the main square. There are stalls selling crafts and all sorts of snacks.

Women show off their national costume in a fiesta parade. They wear embroidered skirts and frilly blouses.

Fireworks explode and firecrackers pop during the May 5 festival.

WORD BANK *mariachi* band of Mexican street musicians. They sing and play violins, guitars, and trumpets.

In full swing

Later in the day, there is a parade in the main square. Everyone is in costume. Some are wearing feathery Indian headdresses. People dance to the music of *mariachi* bands.

Best of all are the fireworks. In Puebla, fireworks are attached to a bull costume. This costume is worn by a man who charges into the crowd. Firecrackers explode everywhere.

Rodeos

Charreadas (rodeos) are held on fiesta days. Cowboys (*charros*) in splendid outfits ride wild bulls or bucking bronco horses. Some show their skill with the **lasso**. They use lassoes to rope bulls and horses as they ride (see left).

lasso long rope with a loop that is used for catching horses and cattle

Important holidays and fiestas

JANUARY 1:
New Year's Day

MARCH 21:
Birthday of Benito Juárez. Juárez was one of Mexico's early presidents

MARCH/APRIL:
Lent and Easter

MAY 5:
Battle of Puebla

SEPTEMBER 15–16:
Independence Day

OCTOBER 12:
Columbus Day

NOVEMBER 1–2:
Day of the Dead

NOVEMBER 20:
Revolution Day

DECEMBER 12:
Feast of Our Lady of Guadalupe

DECEMBER 25:
Christmas Day.

Religion

In the 1500s, the Spanish **conquistadors** came to Mexico. They brought the **Catholic** religion to Mexico. Today, 90 percent of Mexicans are Roman Catholics.

Festivals

Some fiestas celebrate important dates in Mexico's history. Most fiestas, however, are Catholic saints' days. Mexico's best-loved saint is the Virgin of Guadalupe. On the day of the Feast of Our Lady of Guadalupe, there is a big parade in Mexico City.

> ► These skulls are made from chocolate and icing! They are part of the Day of the Dead celebrations.

WORD BANK Catholic to do with the Roman Catholic religion, or a follower of the Roman Catholic religion

Day of the Dead

There are Christian beliefs and Indian beliefs in Mexico. Christian beliefs meet with traditional Indian beliefs in many fiestas. This happens in Mexico's most famous fiesta, the Day of the Dead.

The Day of the Dead is a time when Mexicans remember their dead relatives. Families prepare a feast for the spirits of the dead. People light candles to guide the spirits to their homes. They give sweets and chocolate in the shape of skulls.

Bulls on the loose!

The town of Huamantla in southeast Mexico has a scary festival. It is called *La Noche en que Nadie Duerme*, or "the night when no one sleeps." On this night bulls run loose through the streets. You have to move fast if a bull heads toward you.

23

Everyday Life

It is the morning after the fiesta. Everything is back to normal. People are going to work. Children are going to school.

Mining

Mexico is rich in **minerals** such as gold, silver, zinc, lead, and copper. There are also large stocks of oil and natural gas. Oil and gas are found both on land and in the sea.

Jobs and industry

Puebla's biggest employer is a car factory. Mexico has many factories. They make all kinds of products, such as cars, clothing, and food. U.S. and Japanese companies have set up lots of factories near the U.S. border. These are called *maquiladoras*. *Maquiladoras* employ Mexicans to make their products.

Oil is mined offshore in the Gulf of Mexico.

WORD BANK   mineral substance found in the ground, such as gold, silver, and zinc

Schools

Mexican law says that children must go to school between the ages of six and fourteen. Children of poorer families often do not complete their education. They sometimes have to work instead.

Some children in the countryside live far away from schools. These children go to a *Telesecundaria*. At a *Telesecundaria*, their lessons are transmitted through a television.

This *maquiladora* is in the Mexican border town of Tijuana. The cars and trucks produced there are sold mainly into the United States.

25

Jai alai

Jai alai is a fast game that is a bit like squash. Players use curved rackets to hit a hard rubber ball. The ball can be bounced off the walls of the court. This game came originally from Spain.

So what do Mexicans like to do in their free time? You come across some children playing a game of soccer in an alley.

Soccer crazy

Futbol (soccer) is Mexico's favorite sport. People play it in every town and village. Top matches take place in the Azteca Stadium in Mexico City.

Jai alai is a fast-paced game – the *pelota* (ball) can travel up to 190 mph (290 kph)!

Other sports

Basketball, volleyball, and baseball are also very popular. Bullfighting has been a spectator sport in Mexico for about 500 years. Many people think bullfights are a display of skill and bravery.

Relaxing in Mexico

Whole families enjoy taking evening strolls together. Towns such as Puebla have a lively nightlife with bars, cinemas, and nightclubs.

Mexican *futbol* (soccer) fans enjoy the atmosphere at the 2002 World Cup in Japan.

Travel and Cities

You want to see more of Mexico. The capital, Mexico City, is your next stop. You call in at the tourist office to ask about the best way to travel.

On the road

Mexico has high mountain ranges. This makes it difficult to build roads and railroads across the country. Most major highways and rail routes run north to south. They keep to the **plains** and **valleys**. Buses are one of the best ways of getting about.

Rural transport

You take a bus from Puebla to Mexico City. After Puebla, the road changes. In the countryside, donkeys, oxcarts, motorbikes, and bicycles are used to carry people and heavy loads.

Donkeys are used to help carry firewood in the countryside.

Colorful taxis fill this Mexican street. People in the cities often share taxis.

WORD BANK   plain large, flat area of land

Rail and air

Rail travel is cheap, but not very reliable. The Copper **Canyon** Railroad is one of the few lines that runs smoothly. It has some marvellous views. Some call it "the world's most scenic railroad."

Air travel is a great way to get around Mexico. But it is the most expensive way to travel.

The Copper Canyon Railroad runs for a total of 435 miles (700 kilometers). It crosses 36 bridges and passes through 87 tunnels.

valley lowland between hills or mountains

Sights of the capital

• **Cathedral:**
the largest church in Mexico

• **National Palace:**
site of Mexico's government

• **Templo Mayor:**
remains of an Aztec temple

• **Palace of Fine Arts:**
(see picture below) some of Mexico's greatest art.

Mexico City

Mexico City is one of the largest cities in the world. The bus takes a long time to get you to the city center.

Historic city

Mexico City was founded by the Spanish in 1521. It was built on the ruins of an ancient Aztec capital. Today, Mexico City is a mixture of Spanish-style and modern buildings. Broad avenues run through the city.

WORD BANK **pollution** release of harmful chemicals into the air, ground, or water

Problems

There is a lot to see in Mexico City, but there are problems. Heavy traffic makes driving in the center difficult. It is better to use the underground trains.

Cars and factories cause heavy **pollution** in Mexico City. Pollution causes a blanket of smoky fog, or smog, to hang over the capital. New laws have made it harder for people to use cars in the city. This helps to lower the pollution levels.

That sinking feeling

Mexico City is built on soft, sandy ground. The city sinks 6 inches (15 centimeters) or so every year.

The ground around **Independence** Monument in Mexico City is sinking rapidly.

Mexican cities

Mexico has many other interesting cities to visit. A guide book helps you to decide where to go next.

A typical Mexican city

Guadalajara lies to the west. It is Mexico's second-largest city. The city has a small center with landmarks that date from the 1500s. Guadalajara is the home of *mariachi* music. You can hear it all over the town.

➤ Old Spanish buildings edge the squares of Guadalajara.

WORD BANK   *mariachi* band of Mexican street musicians. They sing and play violins, guitars, and trumpets.

Monterrey or Acapulco?

The busy city of Monterrey is in the northeast. It is surrounded by the Eastern Sierra Madre mountains. There are huge squares with mainly modern buildings.

South of Mexico City lies Acapulco. This is the country's most famous resort. It has sandy beaches and lively nightlife. You decide to hop on a bus to Acapulco.

Divers plunge a massive 130 feet (40 meters) off the cliff at La Quebrada.

Divers of La Quebrada

Acapulco is famous for its daring divers. They plunge into the sea from a steep cliff called La Quebrada. Dives must be carefully timed. Divers need to catch the incoming waves. Otherwise, they will land on the rocks under the surf.

City life

Acapulco is a lively, modern city. It has an old center. Spanish ships used the port in the 1500s. These ships brought silk and spices into the country.

Acapulco's old town has a fort and a main square with some public buildings. Some of these buildings have wall paintings, or **murals,** created by famous Mexican artists.

Mexican artists

Diego Rivera and José Clemente Orozco were famous Mexican artists. Many of their paintings show great events in Mexico's history. Orozco's most famous painting is shown on page 10.

You are here!

MEXICO CITY

Acapulco

0   400 km

0   300 miles

This mural in Acapulco's Presidential Palace is by Diego Rivera. It shows scenes from Mexico's history.

HUELGA

This woman's home in the slums overlooks glamorous Acapulco beach.

Expanding cities

Like many Mexican cities, Acapulco has grown a lot in recent years. Since the 1950s huge numbers of Mexicans have moved from the countryside to the cities. They go to the cities to look for work and a better life. Sadly, many end up jobless. Some live in dirty, overcrowded housing. They live in these **slums** on the edges of the cities.

Harvesting chicle

Tree sap called chicle comes from *sapodilla* trees. *Sapodillas* are grown in Mexican plantations. The sap is collected in little cups. It is then used to make chewing gum.

You catch the bus back toward central Mexico. The road winds up the hills. It passes through farms and forests. Looking back, you can see fishing villages along the blue coast.

Fishing

Fishing has been a major industry in Mexico since the 1960s. The waters around Baja California are rich in fish and shellfish. Along the Gulf of Mexico, shrimping is a big industry.

A worker cuts into a *sapodilla* tree to harvest chicle.

Farming

Most of the Mexican farms you see are small plots. Here farmers grow food for their families. They work with simple tools and plows that are pulled by horses.

There are also big farms that use expensive farm machinery. They grow cotton, wheat, coffee, and sugarcane to sell in other countries.

Forestry

Many of Mexico's forests are being cut down for wood. Cheap timber comes from the pine forests of central Mexico. More valuable woods grow in the rain forests of the southeast.

Ranching

In some parts of Mexico the land is too poor to grow crops. In these areas cattle are kept on huge ranches. In the north, cattle are farmed for their meat. In the south, dairy cattle are reared. Dairy cattle produce milk.

Fishermen bring their catch to a fishing harbor in Baja California.

Country life

The beautiful scenery makes you decide to spend a few days in the countryside. The bus drops you in a tiny village. It is like entering another world.

In the cities most Mexicans wear modern clothes. Here in the country, women wear long skirts, loose blouses, and shawls called *rebozos*. Men wear cotton shirts, trousers, sandals, and **sombreros**.

Farming to eat

Most country people are farmers. Families keep a few animals, such as chickens or a pig. Most of what they farm is for their own needs. They sell any spare food at the local market.

Family life

Grandparents often live with their grown-up children. They help raise the grandchildren. Young people usually live at home until they get married.

sombrero large hat with a wide brim, often worn by Mexican men

Women in the countryside carry their babies in slings made from their shawls.

Land rights

Since the Mexican **Revolution**, most farmland in Mexico has been owned by the group of people who work on it. This shared land is called *ejidos*.

Mexico has many different landscapes. You haven't yet seen the **cactus**-dotted deserts of the north. You haven't seen the mountains of the Sierra Madre or the rain forests of the southeast.

Spectacular ruins

Many tourists aim to visit at least one of Mexico's ancient sites. Among these spectacular ruins are the Mayan temples of the Yucatán. The Mayans were people who lived in southern Mexico about 1,700 years ago.

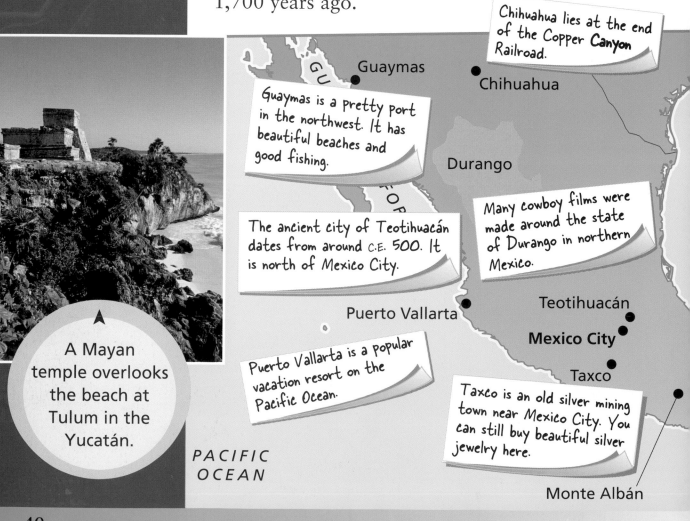

A Mayan temple overlooks the beach at Tulum in the Yucatán.

Chihuahua lies at the end of the Copper Canyon Railroad.

Guaymas

Chihuahua

Guaymas is a pretty port in the northwest. It has beautiful beaches and good fishing.

Durango

Many cowboy films were made around the state of Durango in northern Mexico.

The ancient city of Teotihuacán dates from around C.E. 500. It is north of Mexico City.

Teotihuacán

Puerto Vallarta

Mexico City

Puerto Vallarta is a popular vacation resort on the Pacific Ocean.

Taxco

Taxco is an old silver mining town near Mexico City. You can still buy beautiful silver jewelry here.

PACIFIC OCEAN

Monte Albán

40   **WORD BANK**   cactus thick, prickly plant that stores water in its stem. Cacti grow in dry areas.

Ancient cities

There is also the amazing city of Monte Albán in Oaxaca, southern Mexico. It was built by Zapotec Indians about 2,500 years ago. Experts are not sure who built the pyramids of Teotihuacán near Mexico City. These pyramids were once part of a mighty city.

Flying men of Papantla

Papantla is a town in east-central Mexico. It is the home of the dance of the *voladores* ("flying men"). There are four men in bird costumes with ropes around their waists. They jump from a high pole. The men then circle downward. It is seriously scary!

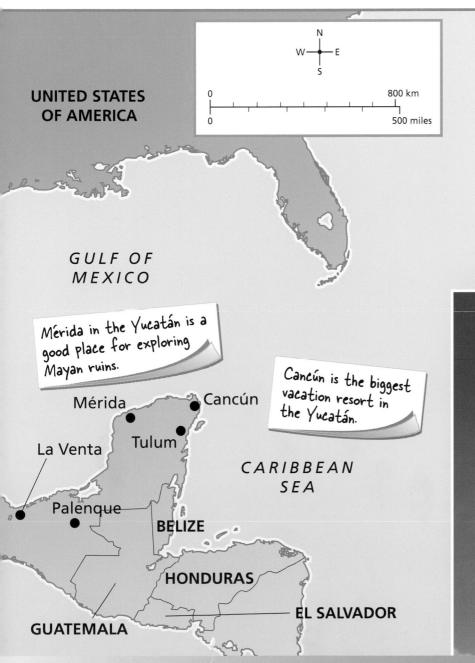

UNITED STATES OF AMERICA

N
W E
S

0   800 km
0   500 miles

GULF OF MEXICO

Mérida in the Yucatán is a good place for exploring Mayan ruins.

Cancún is the biggest vacation resort in the Yucatán.

Mérida   Cancún

La Venta   Tulum

CARIBBEAN SEA

Palenque

BELIZE

HONDURAS

EL SALVADOR

GUATEMALA

Stay or Go Home?

National Parks highlights

• **Agua Azu, Chiapas:** jungle waterfalls

• **Sian Ka'an Reserve, Yucatán:** tropical forests and **mangrove swamps**

• **Cascada de Basaseachic, Chihuahua:** Mexico's second-highest waterfall

• **Copper Canyon:** fantastic **canyon** scenery.

You've seen Puebla, Acapulco, and Mexico City. But Mexico is big. There's still lots to see. Do you hop on a plane and head home? Or do you stay?

Great days out

You make a list of things you really want to do. It includes snorkeling at the coral reefs of the Yucatán. You would also like to explore the underground caves here. You could paddle a kayak between the islands off Baja California. There's so much to do!

Thousands of monarch butterflies cling to a tree in the Michoacán sanctuary.

WORD BANK

mangrove swamp swampy area found along tropical coasts. Mangrove swamps have a huge variety of plants and wildlife.

Wildlife watching

You haven't yet seen much of Mexico's wildlife. At El Rosario in Michoacán you can see monarch butterflies. They fly there all the way from Canada. Scammon's **Lagoon** in Baja California is the place for whale-watching. You can also see monkeys and parrots in the rain forests.

You could go scuba diving off Cozumel Island in the Yucatán.

A gray whale and her calf enjoy the warm waters of Scammon's Lagoon.

Find Out More

World Wide Web

If you want to find out more about Mexico, you can search the Internet. Try using keywords such as these:

- Mexico
- Aztecs
- Day of the Dead

You can also find your own keywords by using words from this book. Try using a search directory such as: yahooligans.com.

Are there ways for a Destination Detective to find out more about Mexico? Yes! Check out the books and movies listed below:

Further reading

Garcia, James. *Cinco de Mayo*. Chanhassen, Minn.: Child's World, 2003.

Green, Jen. *Nations of the World: Mexico*. Chicago: Raintree, 2000.

McCulloch, Julie. *A World of Recipes: Mexico*. Chicago: Heinemann Library, 2001.

Park, Ted. *Taking Your Camera to Mexico*. Chicago: Raintree, 2000.

Parker, Edward. *The Changing Face of Mexico*. Chicago: Raintree, 2002.

Movies

Viva Zapata! (1952)
A film about Emiliano Zapata, the leader of the Mexican Revolution of 1910–1917.

The Treasure of Sierra Madre (1948)
An adventure set in 1920s Mexico. Three men search for gold in the Sierra Madre mountains. They agree to share the gold they find, but they soon turn against each other.

Time Line

around C.E. 300–900
Mayan culture flourishes in southeast Mexico.

1340s
Aztecs found the city of Tenochtitlan (now Mexico City). They rule a large **empire** from this capital.

1519
An army of Spanish **conquistadors** (soldiers) led by Hernán Cortés lands on the Gulf coast.

1521
Spanish conquistadors conquer Tenochtitlan. The Aztec empire becomes part of the Spanish empire.

1540s
The Spanish discover gold in New Spain. Huge amounts of gold and silver are shipped over to Spain.

1810
Miguel Hidalgo calls Mexicans to fight against Spanish rule. His speech begins Mexico's struggle for **independence**.

1821
Mexico wins independence from Spain after eleven years of fighting.

1836
The Mexican territory of Texas wins independence. Texas becomes part of the United States in 1845.

1846–1848
The United States wins a war against Mexico and takes a large area of Mexico.

1855–1864
Benito Juárez, from the Zapotec Indian tribe, is president of Mexico.

1862
France invades Mexico. Mexico defeats France at the Battle of Puebla. The French win later the same year. They make an Austrian archduke, Maximilian, emperor.

1867–1872
Maximilian is overthrown, and Benito Juárez becomes president again.

1876–1911
The dictator Porfirio Díaz rules Mexico.

1910–1917
The Mexican Revolution takes place. Revolutionaries overthrow Díaz's regime.

1917
Mexico has a new form of government.

1929
The National Revolutionary Party (PRM) is formed and wins control of Mexico. In 1946 it becomes the Institutional Revolutionary Party (PRI). It remains in power until the year 2000.

1968
Mexico hosts the Olympic Games.

1985
A major earthquake hits Mexico City.

2000
The PRI loses the elections. President Vicente Fox of the National Action Party is elected.

---

conquistadors Spanish soldiers who conquered the Mexican Indians in the 16th century

Mexico – Facts and Figures

Mexico's flag has three vertical stripes: green, white, and red (left to right). The coat of arms in the center represents a legend. The Aztecs built their capital (now Mexico City) where they saw an eagle sitting on a cactus eating a snake. This is what the coat of arms shows.

People and places

- Population: 104.9 million.
- Mexico City is the oldest capital city in the Americas, and the largest capital city in the world.

Money matters

- Average earnings:
  Men – $13,152
  Women – $4,978.

What's in a name?

- Mexico's original name was *Meshtleeko*. However, the Spanish **conquistadors** found this name hard to say. They changed the name to Mexico instead. The official name of Mexico is *Estados Unidos Mexicanos*, or the United Mexican States.

Food and health

- Mexico introduced chocolate to the world.
- Mexicans drink more bottles of Coca-Cola in a day than any other nationality in the world!

Glossary

active volcano likely to erupt sometime in the future

border imaginary line dividing one country from another

cactus (plural: cacti) thick, prickly plant that stores water in its stem. Cacti grow in dry areas.

canyon deep valley with steep sides that has been formed by running water

Catholic to do with the Roman Catholic religion, or a follower of the Roman Catholic religion

civilization very organized society that has grown in a particular country or region

conquistadors Spanish soldiers who conquered the Mexican Indians in the 1500s

empire group of countries ruled by a single country or ruler

erupt to release lava and ash

hurricane fierce storm with very high winds

independence when a country is free from control of another country

lagoon pool of water by the sea

lasso long rope with a loop that is used for catching horses and cattle

mangrove swamp swampy area found along tropical coasts. Mangrove swamps have a huge variety of plants and wildlife.

mariachi band of Mexican street musicians. They sing and play violins, guitars, and trumpets.

mestizos Mexican people who are a mixture of Indian and European blood

mineral substance found in the ground, such as gold, silver, and zinc

mural painting that has been painted on a wall

peninsula piece of land with water on three sides

plain large, flat area of land

plateau area of high, flat land

pollution release of harmful chemicals into the air, ground, or water

rebellion when a group of people join together to fight against the people who are in power

revolution replacing a government with another one, usually by force

sacrifice someone or something that is killed and offered to a god

slum area populated by very poor people, where the conditions are dirty and overcrowded

sombrero large hat with a wide brim, often worn by Mexican men

tremor small earthquake

valley lowland between hills or mountains

Index